Ideas for Parents of Difficult
Or
Out of Control Teenagers

Helena O'Darity Cromwell

IDEAS FOR PARENTS OF DIFFICULT OR OUT OF CONTROL TEENAGERS

ISBN-10: 978-0-9899161-5-4
ISBN-13: 978-0-9899161-5-8

Publisher: Cross Wise Publishing

http://crosswisepublishing.com

Table of Contents

TWO BOOKS in ONE

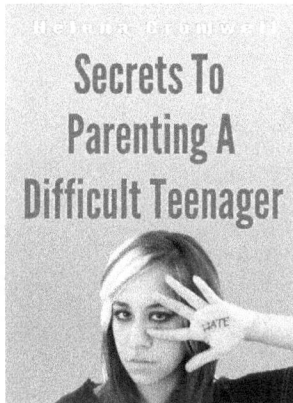

Secrets To Parenting A Difficult Teenager

HELENA O'DARITY

My Teen is Out of Control

A Fast Track Guide for Parents

http://crosswisepublishing.com

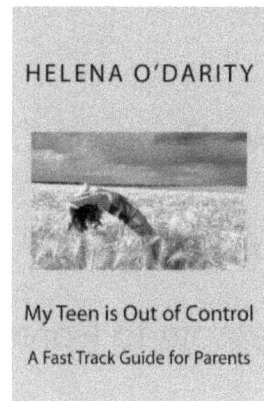

Two Books in One

Parents will find this book to be a compilation of two totally separate books that have a wealth of parenting tips embedded in each of them.

The author takes into consideration that by the time parents get to the point of reaching outside their own knowledge base for ideas, most are pretty well convinced that a problem exists that rises to the intervention level.

Parents may not know exactly what the problem is, so a brief discussion of how to drill down to the discoverability level is presented in each of the guides. However, rehearsing the problem ad nauseous is neither recommended, nor the focus of these parenting guides.

These guides cut to the chase and get down to the business of resolving the problems faced by parents of teenagers who are either problematic, or on their way to becoming problematic.

Readers will find practical ideas and approaches to parenting their teenager that is designed to address both major and minor misbehaviors.

Although these two publications are available individually, they are being offered together so parents have a more complete resource for helping their teen.

Teenagers are individuals with individual problems; hence, there is a wide spectrum of behaviors that present during the teen years. Between these two guides a variety of teen misconduct is presented and challenged from a practical viewpoint.

As in any discipline, to be best equipped, in this case to help a teenager who may have lost their way, interventionist need to broaden their scope and research efforts. The author and publishers of these guides have made them available as a set to simplify the endeavors of such individuals.

Clearly, it's no easy task to raise productive, law abiding citizens in today's culture. This is a world of sensory overload; a world where even good kids do bad things. Therefore, parents who go the extra mile and spend their own time and money on their offspring, making a concerted effort to help their teenager avert a life changing disaster, deserve a big round of applause for at least *trying* to make their child's world a better place.

BOOK ONE

My Teen is Out of Control

A Fast Track Guide for Parents

Helena Cromwell

My Teen is Out of Control

Table of Contents

WITH PRIVILEGE COMES RESPONSIBILITY

Give each child in the household a box or basket and tell them to pretend the house is on fire. Tell them they have 10 minutes to put their most prized possessions in the designated container and return to the living room.

Explain that this is simply a game and that it is nothing to worry about. Once everyone has returned to the living room, or where ever the discussion is to be held one or both of the parents takes out their drivers license and bankcard.

In one hand hold up your drivers license so everyone can see, and in the other hand hold up your bankcard.

Ask your group whom they believe the cards belong to. Most will say they belong to the person whose name is on the card. (If you're lucky enough to have a kid who gets it right off ask him to stick around – tell him you may need his help before the game is over).

The point is that, even though the person whose name is on the card paid for the card, the cards really belong to the issuer - not the person issued the card.

To retain rights to the card the person whose name is on the card must follow rules, regulations, laws and terms of agreement or they could loose their card and all the rights associated with it.

Now it's time for the parent to take back the authority their child may have wrestled away from them.

The Parent needs to explain that even though the things in the box belongs to the person holding it – the adult who paid for the item is the legal owner, and the person using the items has simply been issued the items under certain terms and conditions.

Tell your teens that just as the state or the bank could revoke your use of their card that they issued to you, if you failed to comply with their terms, the same thing can and will happen to them if they fail to comply with your terms.

Reassure them that as long as the rules are followed, neither you nor they have to be concerned with loss of privileges.

As the parent, you may wish to set up a warning system whereby your teen is given up to 3 warnings before action is taken against their item, but they need to understand that you have issued their items in good faith, and that you expect them to respect the rules that are associated with continued use of the items.

Try to end this exercise with a pleasant experience, such as an ice cream party so everyone can feel safe and glad they attended the family meeting.

Note to Parents:
Children really are individuals from conception. It's not always easy for parents to accept the fact their child will have an opinion of their own. Nonetheless, parents still have a duty to teach basic life principles to their children. Along with that though, parents have to come to terms with the fact that sooner or later children are destined to make their own decisions – and the decisions they make are not always decisions the parent agrees with.

Experience tells me that once children reach The adolescent stage of life, parents are there Mostly to support them in the decisions they Make. When they make good decisions you Can applaud, and when they make bad ones You can coach them, and help them discover What the best decision will be the next time They are confronted with a similar situation.

Parents all too often try to soften the blow for Their children. I did that myself. Good parents Try to cushion the blow their child will inevitably Feel due to a wrong decision. Those "hard Knocks" are called consequences.

Some people can observe others' mistakes and Avoid a lot of the trial and error that wrong Decisions bring.

Our two younger sons were much easier to support throughout their teens years than their older Brother was. Sons two and three were more mature and trust worthy as teenagers, and thus able to enjoy many more benefits of the resources we could offer as well.

The bottom line is this. Accept who your child is and what level of maturity they have reached. For example, if your teen is old enough to have a drivers license but is too immature to respect the people who   provide for him, or cannot independently perform age appropriate duties and responsibilities; then you might want to hold up on giving him a 3000-pound car or truck to drive around town in.

Does this mean you will likely be inconvenienced? Yes. Understandably, a teen being able to drive him self is a tremendous asset to a parent, but a teen that is careless or irresponsible with an automobile is likely to bring more than inconvenience to their parents' doorstep.

TEENS NEED PARENTS WHO ARE IN CONTROL

The main point of this chapter is to advise parents to get control of themselves before they try to take control of their teenager. Kids are smart, and they have your number. They know exactly how to "push your buttons."

If you are out of control yourself, you will never be able to be the parent your child needs you to be. If you need anger management classes, then by all means pick up the telephone and find a class. Get on the internet and find and start reading books on how to control your own temper.

You may even need to seek professional help, but don't just sit there doing the same thing you have always done. You cannot explode into a rage and expect your teen to remain calm.

If you don't have an anger issue that needs to be dealt with first, then I will proceed on with a few suggestions that might help you when your child becomes argumentative.

First, something you may want to consider is the fact that your teen wants to communicate with you and will do so on whatever level you allow. So, talk to your teen about things that are non-threatening to them. Find pleasant things to discuss at length with your child.

Discussions about things they are interested in will let them know you enjoy interacting with them. It's called, "making conversation".

Have you ever known anyone who seemed to enjoy a good argument? For some people screaming matches can become addictive. There are chemicals that are released when people are threatened known as the fight or flight reaction.

Some people even get addicted to a feeling of excitement when natural epinephrine is released into their blood stream.

The key to ending the argument before it ever starts is to say what you have to say, and then simply, shut up.

If no really is your answer –then there is no real reason to speak another word. If you can't make yourself "shut up", then you need to physically remove yourself from your teen's airspace.

Go outside if you must, or just go visit a neighbor. Without explanation say, "I'll be right back" and simply leave the premises.

It's extremely difficult to argue with someone who won't converse with you. Teenagers usually try to argue their point "ad nauseous". Some even try to make the parent explain the untoward answer they were given. In other words, they are notorious for trying to argue their parent down on issues they are passionate about.

Be sure to explain that you understand their passion, feelings or urgency. Acknowledging that you "get it" is important, even when you don't agree with them.

One rule of thumb is to be sure that your answer is truly "No" before you give no as an answer,

That you need to think about something is your right as a parent. Snap decisions are not always the best decisions, regardless of the side you take.

Misguided, compassionate parents try to help their teen understand something that clearly, the teen is too immature or else unwilling to understand.

By pass the pleading, begging and possible explosion, and simply give your answer then abruptly end the discussion. Teenagers are smart. Before long your teen will know where the cut off point is.

Whenever you make a new rule be sure to explain to everyone affected, at a time when the rule has no bearing and in full detail the reason for the rule - then stick to it!

You can rest assured that someone will be inconvenienced by the rule, so be prepared to ride through a few rough waves until the rule is firmly established.

Use non-argumentative methods to enforce your rules whenever possible. For example, use the disabling trick. If your rule is no shower past 10pm, then set an alarm for 8pm to warn that the showers will be turned off at 10pm.It's hard to take a shower without hot water.

THE ILL MANNERED TEEN

Teenagers these days face lots of peer pressure to go against the flow, and that includes behaving rudely and crudely. In fact, a teen who is too well mannered is suspect in my opinion.

With that said, it is pleasant to hear teens be courteous to adults and even each other. Normally, by the time a youngster reaches their teen years they know basic manners that are expected in their social circle.

So, teaching manners to teens is usually not as much an issue as enforcing the use of manners.
If your teen is being rude to their family members then parental intervention is a must.

Whatever the rules of conduct are at your house needs to be clear, practiced and extended to everyone.

Your teen needs to understand that just because they are older than their siblings doesn't mean they can be disrespectful to them.

Parents are older than all their children but that doesn't mean they can talk to them like their dogs. That is considered abusive, and for a teen to have an unbridled tongue is the equivalent of abuse.

You may wish to explain it like this. On our highways there are big trucks and there are little trucks. Just because one truck is bigger than the other doesn't give them the right to run over the littler one. The law provides all trucks equal protection on the highway. The same goes for people.

Swearing at anyone in public can get you tossed off the premises. This is simple and basic social etiquette.

The consequences for teens swearing at their family members needs to be consistently applied and severe enough that the teen finds the consequences quite insulting.

Redirecting Rebellion

Rebelling against parental authority is as old as scripture. Remember the Old Testament story of the prodigal son?

Eventually the son saw the error of his ways and came home to a loving and forgiving father. Nonetheless, the son had to learn some pretty hard lessons in the process.

The prodigal son found himself having run out of his inheritance money. Consequently, the wine, women and song was gone as well.

The bewildered son got a reality check, and eventually decided to return home. Since he was reduced to eating and sleeping in the pigs pen he figured out that his father's servants had a better living standard than he did.

So, he returned to his father's house and asked for a servant's portion. Instead he had a loving father who restored him back to being a family member.

To help give a modern day reality check to rebellious teens I make a very strong and strange suggestion to parents. Although this may seem harsh at first, it can actually be fun for all involved.

On a day, and at a time that is convenient for parents (possibly with a little forewarning even) you can call a "disaster drill".

There is more than one point to this drill. Nevertheless, it will serve to uproot your teens from their comfort zone and give them a taste of adventure, as well as enough discomfort to help them appreciate the fact that they have warm, comfortable beds to sleep in at night.

There's nothing like a rude awakening to serve as a distraction, not to mention that it takes energy to be rebellious. Expend some of that energy on learning survival skills in the event of a real emergency and you will have turned a negative into a positive.

I'm sure you have enough imagination to structure the drill to both meet the need to prepare and rehearse for a real life disaster, as well as to accomplish the goal of helping your teen appreciate the strength of having a family to turn to in time of trouble.

You can make the drill as elaborate as you wish, just make sure the children know it will be over in 24 hours.

Better to do something that is not needed than to not do something that was desperately needed. Although teens want to be independent they still desire the security of a family.

Therefore, rebellion that is turning disruptive is not within normal teenage behavior, and as such needs to be addressed from the outside in. Please do not ignore your teen's cry for help. Once a pattern of disruptive behavior has been set it is often near impossible for the target audience of such behavior to stop the momentum without outside help.

Many parents think they don't have the money for a professional counselor. Counselors come in all shapes and sizes.

Many churches have counselors on staff, schools have counselors, and there is usually someone in the extended family the teen likes and trusts.

We sent our teens to church camps that had built in counselors. Put on your thinking cap. I'm sure you'll come up with a creative idea of your own.

A Confident Teen is Less Trouble

The root reason teenagers seek out and participate in risky behaviors is that they desire to be accepted as part of something bigger than themselves.

If you can involve your teen in an extracurricular activity it often meets their need to belong to a group with a common interest. No one has to feel different because they all wear the same uniform – so to speak.

There are all kinds of clubs teens can belong to. Ski clubs, swimming clubs, band, and especially sports teams at school.

The rule I had for my teens was, "You're going to be somewhere doing something, or you're going to be home".

One of the advantages of school activities is that there is adult supervision built in. Look for healthy, adult supervised groups for you child to join.

Not all students are academically gifted, but opportunities for meeting goals, working as a team member and learning to persevere are offered in a variety of other venues.

Parents must start early in helping their child find that healthy place of belonging, beyond the family, whereby their child can excel. Such experiences are vital to the social development of children.

Furthermore, having another entity for the child to be accountable to will benefit even the parents in the long run. I am a firm believer that it takes a village to raise a child.

DIFUSSING THE AGGRESSIVE/VIOLENT
TEENAGER

This chapter is not applicable to every parent who purchases this booklet. However, you may wish to read the chapter for your own information as you may know a parent this chapter would greatly benefit.

Either way, I am including this chapter for informational purposes only, and it is not intended to have stand alone, or therapeutic value.

One of the first things a parent needs to do if they have an aggressive teenager is to put a stop to the aggressive behavior. In some cases the child has learned the behavior from the parent, so taking a look at your own methods for handling your anger and frustrations may be your first step.

I worked as a counselor at a residential center for teens with behavioral disorders for many years. I have personally witnessed instances where professionals deliberately frustrated the teen to a point of aggressive behaviors. I can't recall a single instance where that technique proved to be beneficial to anyone.

If you cannot carry out a discussion calmly with your teenager then you need to bring in outside counsel. I like to think of counseling as parent – teen coaching. Like other coaching, it takes time and hard work to achieve a goal, but if the players stick together they can do it.

The following steps may seem extreme and harsh, but if you have an aggressive teenager the cold hard facts are that you're in a zone that has moved beyond civilized behavior. I suggest you close this book if you're not prepared to face up to that fact.

Know the Law:
1. Everyone in the house needs to realize that domestic violence is no longer tolerated in most jurisdictions within the United States, and as such is a jail able offense.
2. Even making someone fear for their safety is considered fourth degree assault in most states.
3. It is against the law to interrupt the reporting of a crime.
3. It is against the law to falsely report a crime.

Call a family meeting and announce that the aggression has stopped – period. Ask for suggestions of how the family should express their anger or frustrations?

Take even the youngest child's suggestions and write them down. The feelings of everyone in the family need to be acknowledged. You may even want to make a written, Declaration of Peace and have everyone sign it.

The one thing that is the most vital is that everyone agrees there will be no more violence or aggression in your home. Everyone has permission to walk outside to take a time out, but let it be known that where ever and whenever the discussion is taking place the meeting will continue once they return.

Whether or not family meetings lasts until midnight is not important. Meeting the goal that your family will work together to design a plan for dealing with anger and frustrations in a civilized manner is vital.

Tell your teens that the faster you get through the main points (don't try to resolve every little issue at one sitting) the faster the meeting ends. Don't hesitate to use time outs.

Even professional sports teams use "Time Outs" to run the clock out. Use the clock to your advantage to produce fatigue, boredom, and help people realize just how petty some of their complaints really are.

Suggestions You May Want to Try:

1. If you can't talk without yelling at each other then text your feelings to each other
2. Have each person make a list of their grievances
3. Once the meeting begins you may want to ask everyone to hold off on
2 or 3 things from their list for future discussions
4. Allow each person to   read their list
of grievances – be sure to stay calm
5. You may need to invite a respected friend or family member over to act as the chairperson
6. Use parliamentary procedure to add a sense of security, humor, and equality to your meetings
7. Vote for solutions when possible
8. Hold your meeting in a public place where people are forced to behave
9. Always end serious meetings with a fun event or reward that the whole family will stick around for.

NEVER, EVER ambush your family! Always let them know the 3W's. What will be discussed, When and Where the meetings will take place

Give up on the idea that this is a "private" family matter –if the cops get called due to an assault it will be in the local paper under police reports anyway. The purpose of your meeting is to avert that if at all possible.

Going Forward the family bylaws need to state that the police will be called if an aggressive or violent eruption occurs in your home again. Just be sure it's made clear that jail time will be the likely outcome for the offender.

You should further explain that once the police are called there is no point in running because they will simply issue an arrest warrant.

Everyone needs to hang tight so they can tell their side of the story. Officers are trained to sort out the details and can often leave the scene with no one in custody.

Your Teen's Right to Make Choices

My granddaughter recently told me she no longer believes in God. She then asked why she has to go to Church since it's all about something she doesn't even believe in.

My sons attended church every Sunday until the day they moved out of my house, and it was completely without an argument.

Thankfully, we live in a small town and their friends attended the same church so it was simply that they got to be with their friends.

I explained to my granddaughter that I can't make her believe in God, but she still has to go to church because it is the right thing to do. I said, "When you asked me to take you to the mall –I did, and when your sister asked for her sports physical I took her because your mom works during business hours, so you must do what I ask you to do because it is the right thing to do". She complied.

If your teen rebels and chooses to not join the family on Sundays – whether it's to go to services or simply a drive to grandma's house you may be forced to take drastic measures

For example, you may choose to use the same "opting out" technique she used.

When she wants you to take her somewhere of great importance to her – you may need to show her how it feels when her driver refuses to transport her to the event of her choice.

If she tries to circumvent your taking her, you are still within your parental rights to refuse permission for her to go. It's certainly will be to your advantage and add pressure if her event of choice is similar to yours in that it's a regularly scheduled occurrence.

If the aforementioned situation is not feasible for you then you may wish to use the exchange program – which is entirely different from the bargaining teens are so used to.

The exchange program is much like getting a drivers license. There are hoops that have to be jumped through prior to being issued a driver permit.

So, when your teen asks you to do something for them, you reply that after has been completed or complied with, then I will be happy to do for you. Having them meet your terms first is key.

That process is a part of being an adult and will go with your child throughout their entire life. For example, once you finish your degree you get a good job; once you have complied with the banks lending terms (a work history and established credit worthiness) you get a loan; once you can prove you have a job then you can rent an apartment.

In the old days we called this, "don't put the cart in front of the horse".

There's an order for things to occur, and unfortunately too many parents are doing things for their children before the children have earned the right to have it done.

It is certainly true that you can take the horse to the water, but you can't make the horse drink, so don't force them; however, if the horse gets thirsty enough he will eventually drink!

Do This Not That

The following are the final suggestions I have for parents. Be patient and allow your children to:

Experience the consequences of their actions – don't bail them out!

Don't try to give them everything you didn't have as a child

Let them fight some of their own battles – it will help them gain confidence in themselves

Let them learn to appreciate the order of a civilized society

Don't be afraid to address the tough issues just do it calmly and with plenty of forethought.

Remember you are your child's first banker. You paid for everything they have, so if they fall behind on their payments (manners, chores, grades, etc.) you may have to repossess an item or two.
You may even want to give them a set time to redeem their belonging before you auction it off on eBay!

Let your teenager grow up and experience the real world of commerce, exchanging value for value; even if it's just favor for favor (don't lead them to believe THEY can get something for nothing)

God Bless,
Helena Cromwell

SECRETS TO PARENTING
A DIFFICULT
TEENAGER

Helena Cromwell

SECRETS TO PARENTING A DIFFICULT TEENAGER

DEDICATION

As the parent of a son whose teenage years were filled with disruptive – very difficult - behaviors, I want to dedicate this book to those parents who have not given up on their teen. I truly believe research, training and a lot of prayer is what got us through those turbulent years. I also believe, if you'll keep reaching out, and looking up for help the same will work for you.

DISCLAIMER

The material and suggestions contained in this book is presented to its readers as an informational product only. This book is not meant to be a substitute for licensed counsel, including the services of a psychologist, psychiatrist or other mental health professional.

TABLE OF CONTENTS

ALARM BELLS

How Could I Have Not Known?

As the mother of a troubled teen, and many years as a counselor of teens with mental and social disorders – including drug addictions – I can affirm that there are real and varied, "warning signs" that your teen may be having problems. However, for the most
part such "signs" are so blooming subtle that the average parent is rarely prepared to recognize or acknowledge it as anything more than a passing phase.

I remember being highly insulted when my best friend suggested, in no uncertain terms, that my son had, "problems". To me that was absurd. Of course, hindsight is 20/20 and now, 23 years later, I clearly realize that it was true. He had problems that would plague him for decades to come.

I am writing this booklet in hopes of keeping other unsuspecting parents of teens from becoming blind- sided the way I was. I want to provide a basis from which parents can make assessments of their teenager.

Not to alarm parents, but distinguishing between the attention seeking teen, who is just misbehaving to get a rise out of their parents, and one who may be starting to exhibit signs of a more serious nature could mean the difference in life and death.

The purpose of this book is not to try and turn parents into detectives, but to remind parents of how important it is that they not blow off signals that their child may be sending them. Parents, as a rule prefer to believe the best in their children. For many parents, myself included, to admit something is not quite right with their teenager, somehow meant failure as a parent.

Since your teen is the main concern here time is of the essence, so I urge parents to quickly get past the denial, anger and guilt phase. It's absolutely imperative that parents move their focus toward the more productive phase of resolution by identifying the problem and concentrating on the solution

Is There A Problem?

All people have problems to overcome regardless of our stage of development; therefore, the question asked thus far is a rather obtrusive point.

Consequently, the question should be more logically stated as – is there a problem that puts my child at a greater risk for experiencing a life altering roadblock on their path to adulthood?

A fundamental task of responsible parenting is that of keeping yourself alert to potential dangers that can cause your youngster harm.

Hence, you have no reason to bow to the pressure - your teen or anyone else may try to impose upon you for simply asking pointed questions, and spending time talking with your teen about the serious issues of life.

Extremes

An obvious thing that is a tale tell sign of impending problems - regardless of age - is extremes. Whether it's an 18-month-old baby that can't sit up by him self, or a 40-year-old father who prefers to be at work all the time, an extreme is a signal that is worthy of attention.

If you notice that your teenager is shutting himself off from the outside world and just staying in his room unless required to be somewhere else, then that is an extreme that you may want to make note of. Another example is if his grades make a drastic change for the worse, or he starts having friends he doesn't want around his family, money is mysteriously disappearing from your change jar, and/or he no longer has an interest in the extracurricular activities he has always loved, then you may have warning signs of "extremes" worthy of attention.

Alone, most of these extremes may not be worrisome, but once extremes become chained together and a pattern has formed, a parent needs to take notice.

We recently noticed our 8-year-old grandson was taking matches from our kitchen. Upon being questioned he adamantly denied the obvious, so after giving him the fire is dangerous speech our next step is to be a little more aware of his whereabouts and actions. We don't really expect he's going to set the house on fire, but we know to be on our guard – for his sake as well as our own.

TEEN TO ADULTHOOD

Dealing with Difficulties

Just because something is difficult doesn't mean it isn't worth pursuing. For teenagers, beginning the process of separating from their parents is natural, but all too often it becomes a very painful experience for everyone concerned.

Parents may rush to hold their teen back from becoming the inevitable adult they are destined to become, or the teenager may rush toward adulthood a little too fast and furious for their own good.

The temperament of the teen and the parents often makes a huge difference in how smoothly the transition takes place.

Communication between the parent and the child has a tendency to slow or even completely shut down once a person enters their teen years.

Nonetheless, parents need to not fear pushing through the sometimes-obnoxious body language of their teen to let their teenager know they are loved and a valued member of the family.

Body language is a defense mechanism that people of All ages us unconsciously. It's my opinion that too much weight is given to the meaning of body language.

Hopefully, parents will over look their teen's glares, stares and rolling eyes and see the really scared person who lives inside that ever-changing body. Many psychologists purport that an emotionally impaired individual may put up such silent barriers to test your level of concern. Again, make sure your teen knows they are loved.

Life's Pressures

To say that only teenagers deal with peer pressure would be ignoring the social structure of world societies. Peer pressure is exerted on just about every human being on the face of the earth. Social norms are a basic part of any culture and that includes the local high school.

Many adults look back on the peer pressure they experienced in their formative years and vow to never again be subject to such extreme or even repulsive activities. Yet, we see peer pressure everywhere from breast-feeding practices to protocol of the government's heads of state. Let's face it, peer pressure is a fact of life regardless of your age.

Nonetheless, as parents it's our duty to guide our children by teaching them our values, as well as to have self respect. It may be that you need to go the extra mile to support your child's ability to stand up for them self.

Therefore, instilling in your child at a young age that they have a God given duty to be the individual they were created to be, and that they have an obligation to themselves and others make good choices will pay big dividends.

Once they are faced with a difficult situation as teenagers they will be better equipped to resist participating in undesirable activities - which they would likely have preferred to opt out of anyway.

Again, teaching children to make good choices should begin at the earliest age possible, and should include a discussion of the ramifications of making bad choices.

BOOBY TRAPS TO AVOID

Trips, Slips and Falls

In life in general there are many booby traps that people can fall into that will change their lives (almost) forever. That is one of the reasons God gave children parents. It's a parent's job to guide their offspring through the many minefields the child will inevitably encounter along the road to adulthood.

Since the parent has already walked the road to adulthood, they are well aware of possible hazards the average teenager (in any given culture) may face.

Usually the parent is ready and willing to warn their youngster of impending pitfalls; however, some parents may need to hone their communication skills in order to be able to convey such experiences to their child effectively.

Therefore, this chapter is more about coaching the parent in how to address some of the many issues that could throw their teenager off course. The problem is rarely that parents don't know the names of the obstacles their youngster will encounter; the problem is more that parents are not   always equipped to successfully communicate their wisdom to their teen.

Getting Acquainted

As a rule, parents feel they know their child better than anyone else could possibly know them. In my opinion, parents are rightly offended when counselors or well meaning outsiders start trying to tell the parent who their child is.

I'm highly offended when outsiders start trying to tell a child they are the child's "friend". Of course, not always, but most often the child is better served if outsiders point the child toward their parent – who REALLY is their highly invested friend!

With that said, let me ask you this. Does your teenager know who he is? Does he feel lost, or does he have a firm grip on what his purpose in life is and what direction he wants to take once he reaches adulthood?

If your teen has not come to terms with who he is and what his purpose in life is, then he will likely be a lot more vulnerable to falling into the many negative traps he encounters along the road to adulthood.

Helping your teenager solidify his character by supporting his goals to become a person with integrity will pay big dividends in the long run for both of you, the parent and the child.

It's essential that teenagers have had a solid foundation of knowing how to make good choices and then having the conviction to stand by the choice they made.

Parents can help their child develop a sense of right and wrong, as well as a sense of purpose and direction by not only making sure your child is exposed to healthy groups (such as scouting and extracurricular opportunities at school), but by setting the example of getting involved in community service and other purpose driven activities as well.

Parents who set a good example for their child early by teaching how to resolve conflicts calmly and skillfully will reap the benefit during the teen years. Such training helps children learn how to handle their own anger and frustrations, without using violence, further down the road.

Additionally, parents can lay the foundation of good, moral character by living a life that doesn't always choose the easy road. Make sure your teenager sees you apologize for a mistake, or being a person who keeps your word, for instance.

The old saying, "character is better caught than taught" is still true today. The stronger your teens character the less likely they will fall into a social trap that could alter their life forever.

Dealing With Missed Steps

There was only one perfect person – and they killed him, so that means the rest of us will have to learn to deal with our shortcomings as we move through life. My point is, we mere mortals are only human and that means we all make mistakes.

Learning to take the proper steps to get past our offenses with the least amount of collateral damage is not a science – it's an art.

A major tool a parent can use to help their teen stay on course is to make sure the teenager has set both long and short-term goals for himself.

Parents can sit down with their teen and LISTEN to the aspirations their child has for the future. This is not a place for the parent to try to inject his or her own opinions.

The parent needs to go mute and try to hear their child's heart in what they desire for their future. Parents need to be open to a broad range of acceptable and less acceptable goal setting at this point. The whole point of this interaction is to determine if your child has thought about their future in a serious way or not.

Have your child write out (on paper) their long-term goals, and then have them identify their short-term goals. It's best if parents do this exercise as early in the teen years as possible. This tool alone can be an invaluable help to a parent who wants to keep their child on track during their trip from childhood to adulthood.

Once you have the child's goals in writing it will give you a focal point in a wide variety of situations. For example, if your child's grades start to drop you can revisit the goals document and discuss what steps need to be taken to get back on track.

If your teenager is struggling in school – either academically or socially – try to calmly get to the bottom of the problem. For teenagers, school is a vital part of their lives. Their success in high school often sets the direction they will head into as adults. Therefore, don't hesitate to invest time and money into your teenager's high school career.

BEHAVIORAL PROBLEMS

The Root of the Problem

If your teenager suddenly appears to have lost their way and begins to exhibit behavior that is abnormal for them, then you will need to be able to skillfully ramp up your observations. In order to do so you will need to know basics of things like, symptoms of teenage depression.

Symptoms of teen depression are not limited to just the following, but some standard behaviors include: excessive sadness or moodiness, unexplained weight changes, loss of interest in school or social activities, excessive absences from school, unexplained physical aches and pains, sudden episodes of rage or guilt, decreased ability to concentrate, and even the choice, or preoccupation with dark color schemes for clothing, artwork and even decorations for their bedroom.

Assuming you're already on top of knowing who your child's friends are and where they spend their free time, this discussion will focus on behavior changes that are associated with a limited set of problems your teenager may be experiencing.

Most children are diagnosed with Attention Deficit Disorder, and other learning disabilities early on in the educational process. That is not to say that your child may not have such diagnoses, but the focus of this booklet will be to make parents more aware of the more affective disorders teens are susceptible to.

Affective disorders are commonly known as "mood disorders". They are things such as depression and anxiety. The discussion of bipolar disorder (that is also an affective disorder) is beyond the scope of this booklet.

Nonetheless, if a teen is experiencing major mood swings it is highly recommended, that parents seek medical attention for their teenager in order to rule out such a serious disorder.

Teen depression exhibits itself in several different ways depending on the person and the severity of the episode.

Parents may not realize the impact that stress can have on their growing teenager. We often hear the term, "Drama Queen". To the most "normal" teenager having things go wrong in their life can be extremely stressful.

If a stressful event is coupled with the feeling that there is little to nothing the teen can do to change the situation, then the result may be fertile ground for the their feeling helpless.

The more the teen dwells on the situation, without adult counsel and intervention the more likely they are to fall into an unhealthy mood that may lead toward depression.

It doesn't always take an earth-shaking event to put a teenager into a mild depression. However, parents need to be especially mindful of drastic life changes and events that affect or threaten their teenagers' feelings of security.

Such events may include, but not be limited to events like long distance moves, marital problems between the parents, death of a friend or relative, or even the passing of a favorite pet.

Recognizing how fragile some teenager's psyche is, when there is a traumatic event in a school or community, that directly affects students, modern school districts readily provide professional counseling as a precautionary measure.

Additionally, long term monitoring of academic, social and energy levels of teenagers, who have experienced traumatic events in their lives, have proven to pay off in terms of mitigating further disruption to schools and communities.

Other considerations that may affect teenagers and impair their brain development is issues such as fetal alcohol syndrome, traumatic brain injury (even mild concussions from sports) and possible chemical imbalances from everything from undiagnosed medical conditions to recreational drug use.

The most important thing is that parents keep an open mind and be determined to intervene on their child's behalf – regardless of what the problem is.

If your teenager is diagnosed with depression, by a mental health professional, the treatment may include regular therapy sessions or even medication if the depression sets in for an extended period of time.

In such an event parents can best help their depressed teen by first recognizing that the teenager is in need of treatment, and then by being persistent in following up with whatever treatment is prescribed for their child.

Usually depression will pass on its own, but be aware if your teenager is experiencing prolonged episodes of depression.

We wont go into all the ramifications of prolonged depression, but I can tell you we had a close call with attempted suicide with our son so don't blow it off if you suspect depression in your teen.

If Not Depression - then WHAT?

Factors that cause behavioral problems can be as complex as diagnosed or undiagnosed behavior disorders, or as simple as normal, healthy teenage rebellion. Consequently, the "root" of teenaged behavioral problems can be wide and varied.

Parents most often find their teens' behavioral problems manageable, but when their teenager is completely out of control it is imperative that professional help be brought in.

Regardless of the cause, if behavioral disorders are caught early enough parents can most likely help their child effectively deal with the symptoms. The cause of interruptive behavior is not always isolated, but mental health professionals can be of great assistance when the family cannot manage their teen's behaviors on their own.

If you're confident that your teen is not exhibiting symptoms of a behavioral disorder, but is just attention seeking then, by all means give him the attention he craves.

Additionally, try to redirect his energy into a healthy activity such as extracurricular activities at school, church youth groups, summer camps, a part time job, or possibly community service where he will be made to feel appreciated for his efforts.

We all like to feel acknowledged, and that is especially important for children. They will go to great lengths to get an adults attention, so the sooner you meet their need for your attention the better the outcome will be.

We've identified a few possible issues your teenager could be facing. However, the point I most want to stress to parents is that behaviors are simply symptoms of deeper issues.

It's often the method that a teen chooses to express their feelings of anger, rebellion, confusion, frustration or whatever that causes parents to flip their wig, start the loud lecturing and get side tracked.

In the bigger picture the wise parent focuses on the solution – not the problem. Therefore, the best defense a parent has against unacceptable behaviors is conversation. You must keep in mind that your ability to effectively communicate with your child is absolutely essential if you want to dig down deep into their heart and soul and find the "root" of their problem.

The worst of behaviors is, at the end of the day, nothing more than a symptom of a more serious problem. It's up to you, as the parent to discern whether or not you can resolve the problem on your own or whether you need to seek outside help.

When you are sincere about communicating with your child you will open your ears, and tape your mouth closed. Remember, your teen no more wants to hear what you have to say than you want to hear what they have to say. Each of you thinks you know the solution for a quick fix to the problem.

The REAL problem is – you don't know what the problem is until you first listen to your teenager. Your teen is likely poorly skilled at expressing his feelings and thoughts, so stay calm and be patient. You have to treat this session with your child as if you're an investigator trying to get all the facts.

It's unacceptable for an investigator to put words in a witness's mouth. They repeatedly use terms such as, "and then what happened?"

They use open-ended questions that do not require a yes or no answer. "So, what do you think would help?" or "So, what would you like me to do?" A good investigator's initial purpose is to gather as much information as they can.

Only after that do they move on to trying to put the pieces of the puzzle together. I can't stress enough, that the questioning phase of an investigation is a total separate step to that of analyzing the information gathered.

Investigators repeat back what they think they are hearing with phrases like, "so, if I'm understanding you correctly... or just to be clear what your telling me is...." Another technique is to simply repeat ONE word of something they've said to get them to elaborate more on what they're trying to say.

This is your child, they will never stop being your child – as the saying goes, you've been given a lifetime sentence without time off for good behavior. In other words, you're in this for the long haul.

Try to be respectful, try to keep your focus on one issue or grievance at a time and most of all try to be objective and DON'T EXPLODE, regardless of what you hear.

Believe me, I completely understand that you're likely dealing with a kid who has little appreciation for the blood, sweat and tears you've invested into his life, but your staying calm will pay higher dividends in the long run.

Take heart, these teen years will pass, so stay in there and don't give up. Keep in mind that sometimes teens will respond better to outsiders. You have to make the call of whether or not you need reinforcements, but experience tells me that communicating with the child (inside the almost adult body) is your greatest challenge. Once you master real communication – all the other problems will more quickly get resolved.

CONCLUSION

http://crosswisepublishing.com

All adults have walked the road that takes a person from childhood to adulthood. We have all tripped, slipped or possibly even fallen by the way side and needed someone to come along beside us and help us up.

I said that to encourage you that all parents face some type of challenge when getting their teenager through those often-turbulent years.

You may or may not see what others are going through with their teens, but trust me everyone has problems. If a parent has been blessed enough to learn the importance of teaching their child to communicate with them whether or not things are going well, then that parent may have a little easier road than most.

Nonetheless, the issues of life challenge us all. The ability to effectively communicate our position on a particular issue, our pain in a particular circumstance, or even what challenges us in life in general is key to our happiness.

If you can effectively communicate your position on an issue you can make inroads into the hearts and lives of the people in your circle of influence. For example, almost all job descriptions ask for good communication skills.

Therefore, if there is only one take away from this booklet I'd like to think it is one of having gained a better perspective on how important it is to communicate openly and honestly with your teenager.

A difficult teen is not one that is completely out of control. A difficult teenager is one that is a challenge for their parents, but the outcome is usually positive if the parent has just a little bit of coaching along the way.

About the Author

Helena Cromwell is the mother of 3 adult sons, and the grandmother of 13. Helena holds a B.S. in Health, a Masters Degree and a Graduate Certificate in Industrial Hygiene from Tulane University. Not only did she spend 5 years in the trenches with her own difficult teenager, but she is the recipient of the prestigious Guy Long Award for her work as a mental health professional at Alaska's largest treatment center for teens with behavioral disorders. Helena believes children are a gift from God and that life at all stages of development is precious.

BOOKS BY HELENA CROMWELL

My Teen is Out of Control

CONCLUSION

By presenting these two booklets as a set, the author hopes her readers discovered a broader perspective and greater encouragement than either book offered in solitaire. These writings were meant to serve anyone responsible for the parenting of a teenager who may be prone to exhibiting radical or defiant behaviors.

Understandably, the teen years are filled with extreme changes which some youths cope with better than others. Not only are their bodies changing, but also societies expectations of their entire existence changes. Although the vast majority of teens eagerly rise to the occasion, the sheer economic, legal and interpersonal transformations, that directly impact their lives, may cause some individuals to make less than desirable choices.

Further, it is no wonder that during these short, often-tumultuous years many parents find themselves facing greater challenges than any other time in their child's rearing. Please know that this author strongly supports the parent's efforts to reach out for help.

Therefore, it is our hope that our readership will continue to reach out, beyond the scope of even this writing, for new ideas and assistance as they guide and direct their youngster through the transition from childhood to adulthood.

This author believes strongly that parents know their child better than most anyone else possibly could. Hence, our readership is encouraged to stay the course, and at the end of day, use their own best judgment where their child is concerned.

Finally, parents are advised to use this material as only a small part of their plan to move their teenager toward the goal post of becoming a responsible, law abiding and productive citizen of the "real world", where a note from your mother does little good.

God Speed.
Helena Cromwell